PORTUGUESE

COLORING BOOK

FOR KIDS

This book belongs to

_____

- -

▬▬▬▬▬▬▬▬▬▬▬▬▬▬▬▬▬▬▬▬▬

Jacaré
Alligator

Ursa
Bear

Pássaro
Bird

Camelo

Camel

Capivara

Capybara

Gata
Cat

Galinha

Chicken

Vaca

Cow

Veado

Deer

Portuguese Animals Word Search

Directions: Find and circle the portuguese words. Look for words in all directions: top-down, left-right and diagonal.

R	T	O	N	H	G	O	E	L	E	F	A	N	T	E	V	T	C
A	O	I	E	B	I	E	A	G	O	U	I	A	E	B	G	O	O
U	N	E	R	Y	R	S	T	F	N	D	E	F	R	Y	F	N	E
R	F	F	A	M	A	A	K	M	F	C	F	R	A	M	M	F	L
S	P	G	T	F	F	K	F	K	M	F	V	T	T	F	K	P	H
O	F	C	K	L	A	D	P	A	A	G	A	U	K	L	A	F	O
K	X	Y	A	I	H	F	K	G	C	H	C	A	F	I	G	X	H
A	R	U	P	V	Y	G	A	O	A	J	A	Q	P	Q	O	R	Y
V	U	H	K	Y	A	E	V	L	C	E	H	I	K	Y	L	U	V
H	Z	B	A	C	A	L	H	A	O	P	B	P	A	C	A	Z	Q
P	Z	V	V	C	I	I	O	O	Z	F	V	P	V	M	O	Z	I
P	I	C	H	M	X	A	P	I	P	O	R	C	O	M	I	I	X

CAVALO	**ELEFANTE**	**MACACO**	**URSO**
HORSE	ELEPHANT	MONKEY	BEAR

GIRAFA	**COELHO**	**PORCO**	**VACA**
GIRAFFE	RABBIT	PIG	COW

Cachorro

Dog

Name: _____ **Date:** _____

How am I feeling?

Directions: Trace the word and then draw the emotion.

happy

Feliz

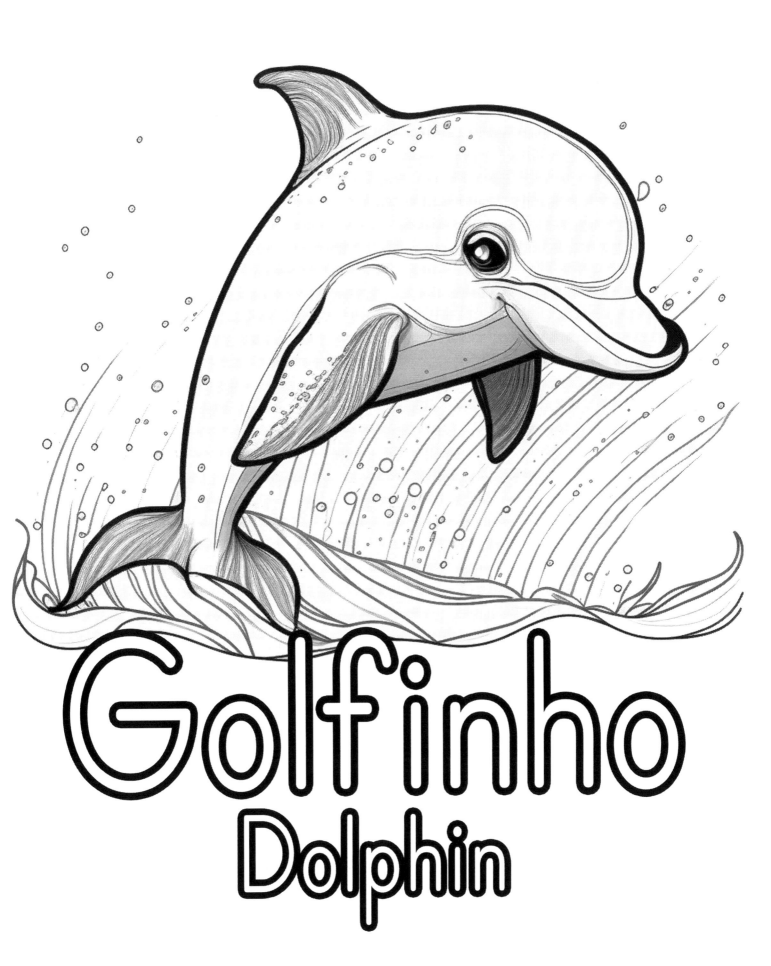

Golfinho
Dolphin

Burro
Donkey

How am I feeling?

Directions: Trace the word and then draw the emotion.

happy

Feliz

Pato

Duck

Elefanta
Elephant

Peixe

Fish

Portuguese Vegetables Word Search

Directions: Find and circle the portuguese words. Look for words in all directions: top-down, left-right and diagonal.

```
R  O  O  N  H  G  O  E  L  E  F  B  A  T  A  T  A  C
A  N  I  E  B  I  E  A  G  O  U  I  A  E  B  G  O  O
P  E  P  I  N  O  S  T  F  N  C  E  N  O  U  R  A  E
R  O  F  A  M  A  A  K  M  F  C  F  R  A  M  M  F  S
S  N  G  B  F  F  K  F  K  M  F  V  T  T  F  K  P  P
O  F  C  A  R  A  D  P  A  A  G  A  U  K  L  A  F  I
K  X  Y  L  I  Ó  F  K  G  C  H  C  A  F  I  G  X  N
A  R  U  F  V  Y  C  A  O  A  J  A  Q  P  Q  O  R  A
V  U  H  A  Y  A  E  O  L  C  E  B  O  L  A  L  U  F
H  Z  B  C  C  A  L  H  L  O  P  B  P  A  C  A  Z  R
P  Z  V  E  C  I  I  O  O  I  F  V  P  V  M  O  Z  E
A  L  H  O  M  X  A  P  I  P  S  R  C  O  M  I  I  X
```

CEBOLA	**BRÓCOLIS**	**ESPINAFRE**	**PEPINO**
ONION	BROCCOLI	SPINACH	CUCUMBER

ALFACE	**BATATA**	**CENOURA**	**ALHO**
LETTUCE	POTATO	CARROT	GARLIC

Raposa
Fox

Portuguese Fruit Word Search

Directions: Find and circle the portuguese words. Look for words in all directions: top-down, left-right and diagonal.

R	O	O	M	A	Ç	Ã	E	L	E	F	B	G	G	A	T	A	C
A	N	I	E	B	I	E	A	G	O	U	I	A	E	B	G	O	O
P	I	R	I	N	E	S	T	F	N	C	G	O	I	A	B	A	P
Ê	O	F	A	M	A	A	K	M	F	C	F	R	A	M	M	F	S
S	N	G	B	F	F	A	B	A	C	A	X	I	T	F	K	P	P
S	F	C	A	M	A	D	P	A	A	G	A	U	K	L	P	F	I
E	X	Y	L	I	A	F	K	G	C	H	C	E	F	I	E	X	N
G	R	U	F	V	Y	N	A	O	A	E	A	Q	P	Q	R	R	A
O	U	H	A	Y	A	E	G	L	C	E	R	I	K	Y	A	U	F
H	Z	B	C	C	A	L	H	A	O	P	B	E	A	C	A	Z	R
P	Z	V	E	C	I	I	O	E	I	F	V	P	J	M	O	Z	E
B	C	O	C	O	X	A	P	I	P	S	R	C	O	A	P	V	T

MAÇÃ	**GOIABA**	**PÊSSEGO**	**PERA**
APPLE	GUAVA	PEACH	PEAR

COCO	**CEREJA**	**ABACAXI**	**MANGA**
COCONUT	CHERRY	PINEAPPLE	MANGO

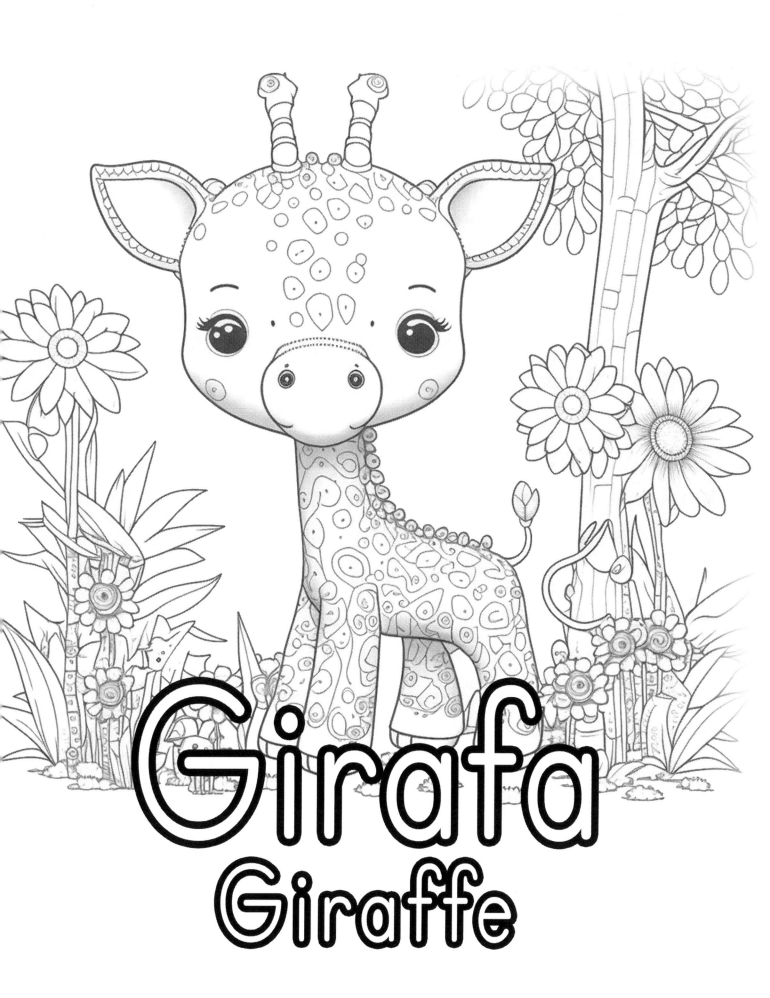

Girafa

Giraffe

Bode
Goat

Hipopótamo
Hippopotamus

Cavalo
Horse

How am I feeling?

Directions: Trace the word and then draw the emotion.

sad

Triste

Leão
Lion

Leão
Lion

Lagarto
Lizard

Portuguese Family Word Search

Directions: Find and circle the portuguese words. Look for words in all directions: top-down, left-right and diagonal.

R	I	O	N	H	G	O	E	L	V	O	V	Ó	G	A	T	A	C
A	N	R	E	B	I	E	A	G	O	U	I	A	E	B	G	P	O
E	I	R	M	N	E	S	T	F	N	C	E	N	O	U	R	A	P
E	O	F	A	Ã	A	A	M	M	F	C	F	R	A	M	M	I	S
S	N	G	B	F	O	K	Ã	K	M	F	V	T	T	F	K	P	P
B	F	C	A	E	A	D	E	A	A	G	A	U	K	L	A	F	I
T	I	O	L	I	S	F	K	G	C	H	C	E	F	I	G	X	N
A	R	U	F	V	Y	C	A	O	A	J	A	T	P	Q	O	R	A
V	U	H	A	I	A	E	E	L	C	E	H	I	K	Y	L	U	F
H	Z	B	C	R	A	L	H	L	O	P	B	A	A	C	A	Z	R
P	Z	V	E	M	I	I	O	E	I	F	V	P	V	M	O	Z	E
B	L	H	E	Ã	X	A	P	I	P	S	R	C	O	V	O	V	Ô

MÃE	**IRMÃO**	**TIA**	**VOVÓ**
MOM	BROTHER	AUNT	GRANDMA

PAI	**IRMÃ**	**TIO**	**VOVÔ**
DAD	SISTER	UNCLE	GRANDPA

Camundongo
Mouse

Coruja
Owl

Portuguese Emotions Word Search

Directions: Find and circle the portuguese words. Look for words in all directions: top-down, left-right and diagonal.

```
R O O A N I M A D O F B G G A T A C
A N I E B I E A G O U I T Í M I D O
E I R I N E S T F N C P E R U Y A P
E O F F E L I Z M F C C R A M M F S
S N G B F F K F K M F V O T F K P P
B C C A E A D P A A G A U N L A F I
K A Y L I T F K G C H C E F F G X N
A N U F V R C A B R A V O P Q U R A
V S H A Y I E E L C E H I K Y L S F
H A B C C S L H L O P B P A C A Z O
P D V E C T I O E I B O B O M O Z E
B O H E M E A P I P S R C O V P V T
```

FELIZ	ANIMADO	CANSADO	TRISTE
HAPPY	EXCITED	TIRED	SAD

BRAVO	CONFUSO	TÍMIDO	BOBO
ANGRY	CONFUSED	SHY	SILLY

Panda
Panda

Pinguim

Penguin

Porca
Pig

How am I feeling?

Directions: Trace the word and then draw the emotion.

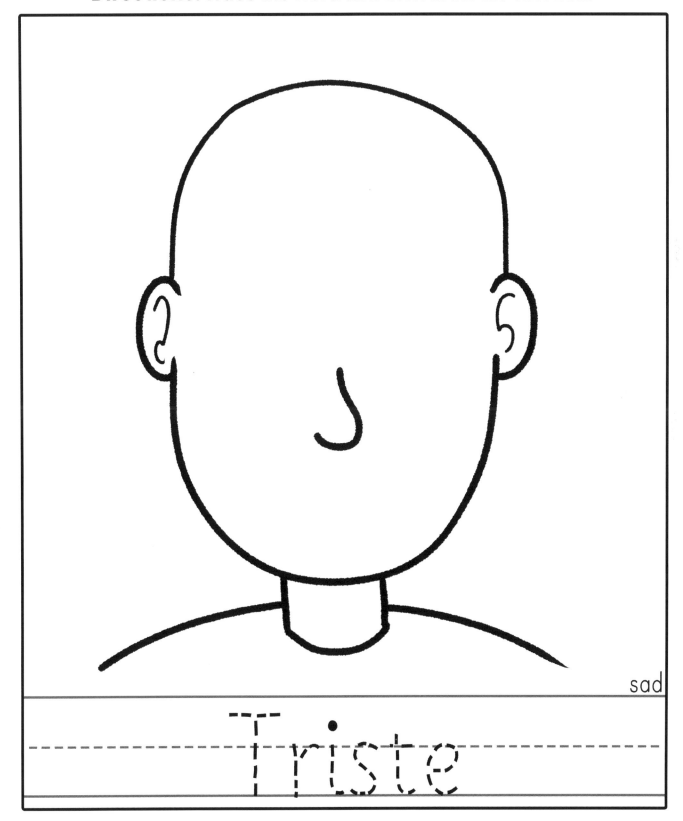

sad

Triste

Coelha
Rabbit

Guaxinim
Raccoon

Portuguese Clothes Word Search

Directions: Find and circle the portuguese words. Look for words in all directions: top-down, left-right and diagonal.

```
R O O N J A Q U E T A B G G A T A R
A V I C B I E A G O U I A E B G O O
E E R I A E S T F N C P E R U Y A P
E S F A M M A K M F C B O T A S F S
S T G B F F I F K M F V T T F K P P
B I C A E A D S A A G A U K L A S I
K D Y L I S F K A C H C E F I G A N
A O U M V Y C A O A J A Q P Q O P A
V U H E Y A E C A L Ç A I K Y L A F
H Z B I C A L H L O P B P A C A T R
P Z V A C I I C H A P É U V M O O E
B L H S M X A P Q P S R C O V P S T
```

BOTAS	CAMISA	JAQUETA	CALÇA
BOOTS	SHIRT	JACKET	PANTS

MEIAS	SAPATOS	VESTIDO	CHAPÉU
SOCKS	SHOES	DRESS	HAT

Tubarão
Shark

Carneiro

Sheep

Name: _____ **Date:** _____

How am I feeling?

Directions: Trace the word and then draw the emotion.

angry

Brava

Cobra
Snake

Tigresa
Tiger

Portuguese Colors Word Search

Directions: Find and circle the portuguese words. Look for words in all directions: top-down, left-right and diagonal.

```
R O O V E R M E L H O B G G A T A C
R N I E B I E A G O U I A E B G O O
O I R I N R O S A N C P E A U Y A P
X O A A M A A K M F C F R Z M M F S
O N G M F F K F K L F V T U F K P P
B F C A A A D P A A A A U L L A F I
K X Y L I R F K G C H R E F I G C N
A R U F V V Y E A O A J A A P Q O I A
V U H A Y A E L L C E H I N Y L N F
H Z B C C A L H O O P B P A J A Z R
P V E R D E I O E I F V P V M A A E
B L H E M X A P I P S R C O V P V T
```

AZUL	**VERMELHO**	**AMARELO**	**ROSA**
BLUE	RED	YELLOW	PINK
VERDE	**LARANJA**	**ROXO**	**CINZA**
GREEN	ORANGE	PURPLE	GRAY

Tigre
Tiger

Tucano
Toucan

Baleia
Whale

Lobo
Wolf

Name: _____ **Date:** _____

How am I feeling?

Directions: Trace the word and then draw the emotion.

angry

Bravo

Zebra

Zebra

Portuguese
Color the Alphabet

Avestruz
Ostrich

Name: _____   **Date:** _____

Portuguese
Color the Alphabet

Baleia
Whale

How am I feeling?

Directions: Trace the word and then draw the emotion.

tired

Cansado

Name: _____ Date: _____

Portuguese
Color the Alphabet

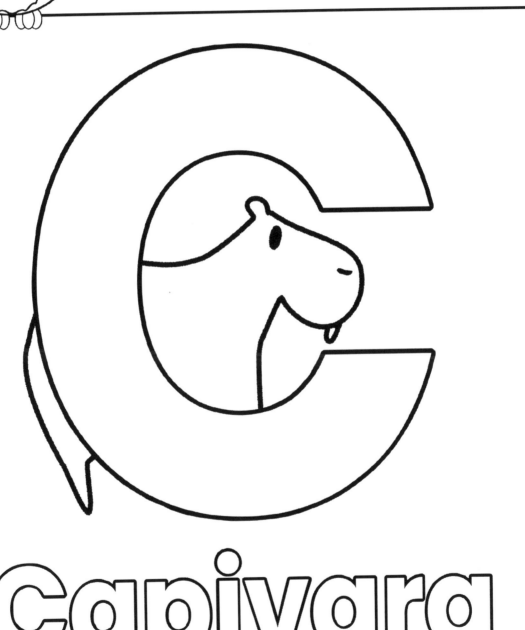

Capivara
Capybara

Portuguese
Color the Alphabet

Doninha

Weasel

Name: _____   Date: _____

Portuguese
Color the Alphabet

Elefante
Elephant

Name: _____   **Date:** _____

Portuguese Body Parts Word Search

Directions: Find and circle the portuguese words. Look for words in all directions: top-down, left-right and diagonal.

R O O N H G O E C E F B G N A R I Z
A O I E B I E A A O U I A E B G O O
E I M I N E S T B N C P E R U Y A P
E O F B M A A K E F C F D A M M F S
S N G B R F K F L M F V E T F K P P
B F C A E O D P O A G A D K L A F I
K X Y L I S F K G C H C O F I G X N
A R U F V Y C A O A J A Q P Q O R A
V U H J O E L H O C E H I K Y L U F
H Z B C C A L H L O P B P A B O C A
P Z D E N T E S E I F V P V M O Z E
B L H E M X A P I P S R O L H O V T

NARIZ
NOSE

JOELHO
KNEE

OMBRO
SHOULDER

DEDO
FINGER

BOCA
MOUTH

CABELO
HAIR

DENTES
TEETH

OLHO
EYE

Portuguese
Color the Alphabet

Name: _____ Date: _____

Flor
Flower

Portuguese
Color the Alphabet

Gato
Cat

Name: _____ **Date:** _____

Portuguese
Color the Alphabet

Hipopótamo

Hippopotamus

How am I feeling?

Directions: Trace the word and then draw the emotion.

tired

Cansado

Name: _____ Date: _____

Portuguese
Color the Alphabet

Iguana
Iguana

Name: _____ Date: _____

Portuguese
Color the Alphabet

Jacaré

Alligator

Name: _____ **Date:** _____

Portuguese
Color the Alphabet

K

Kiwi

Kiwi

Portuguese Solar System Word Search

Directions: Find and circle the portuguese words.
Look for words in all directions: top-down,
left-right and diagonal.

```
R U R A N O O E L E F B G G A T A C
A N I M B I E A J Ú P I T E R G O O
E I R I E E S T F N C P E R U M A P
E O F A M R A K M F S F R A M A F S
V N G B F F C F K M F A T T F R P P
Ê F C A E A D Ú A A G A T K L T F I
N X Y L I S F K R C H C E U I E X N
U R T E R R A A O I J A Q P R O R A
S U H A Y A E E L C O H I K Y N U F
H Z B C C A L H L O P B P A C A O R
P Z V E C I I O E I F V P V M O Z E
B L H E N E T U N O S R C O V P V T
```

TERRA	**NETUNO**	**JÚPITER**	**MARTE**
EARTH	NEPTUNE	JUPITER	MARS
URANO	**SATURNO**	**MERCÚRIO**	**VÊNUS**
URANUS	SATURN	MERCURY	VENUS

Name: _____ Date: _____

Portuguese
Color the Alphabet

Leão
Lion

Portuguese
Color the Alphabet

Macaco
Monkey

Name: _____   Date: _____

Portuguese
Color the Alphabet

Navio
Ship

How am I feeling?

Directions: Trace the word and then draw the emotion.

excited

Animado

Portuguese
Color the Alphabet

Ovelha
Sheep

Name: _____ **Date:** _____

Portuguese
Color the Alphabet

Pato
Duck

Portuguese
Color the Alphabet

Queijo

Cheese

Name: _____ Date: _____

Portuguese Weather Word Search

Directions: Find and circle the portuguese words. Look for words in all directions: top-down, left-right and diagonal.

```
R O O N H C A L O R F B G G A T A C
A N N E B I E A G O U I N E B G O O
C I E I E E S T F N C P U R U Y A A
H O V A M N A K M F C F B A M M F R
U N A B F F S F K M F V L T F K P C
V F N A E A D O A A G A A K L A F O
O X D L I S F K L C H C D F I G X -
S R O F V Y C A O A J A O P Q O R Í
O U H A F R I O L C R H I K Y L U R
H Z B C C A L H L O P A P A C A Z I
P Z V E C I I O E I F V D V M O Z S
B L V E N T A N D O S R C O V P V T
```

CALOR	ENSOLARADO	NUBLADO	CHUVOSO
HOT	SUNNY	CLOUDY	RAINY

FRIO	ARCO-ÍRIS	VENTANDO	NEVANDO
COLD	RAINBOW	WINDY	SNOWING

Name: _____ Date: _____

Portuguese
Color the Alphabet

R

Rato
Rat

Portuguese
Color the Alphabet

Sol
Sun

Name: _____ **Date:** _____

Portuguese
Color the Alphabet

Tigre
Tiger

Portuguese
Color the Alphabet

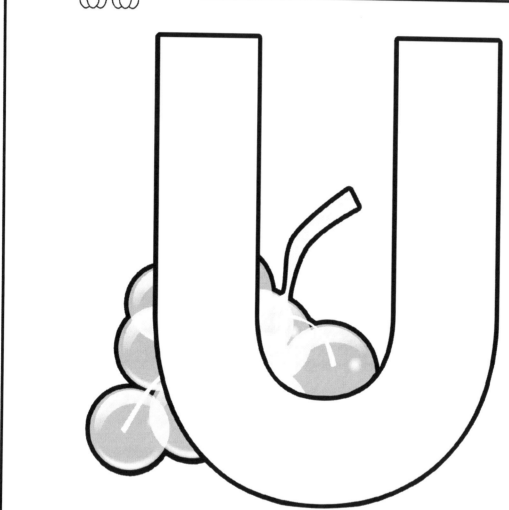

Uvas

Grapes

Name: _____   Date: _____

Portuguese
Color the Alphabet

Vaca

Cow

How am I feeling?

Directions: Trace the word and then draw the emotion.

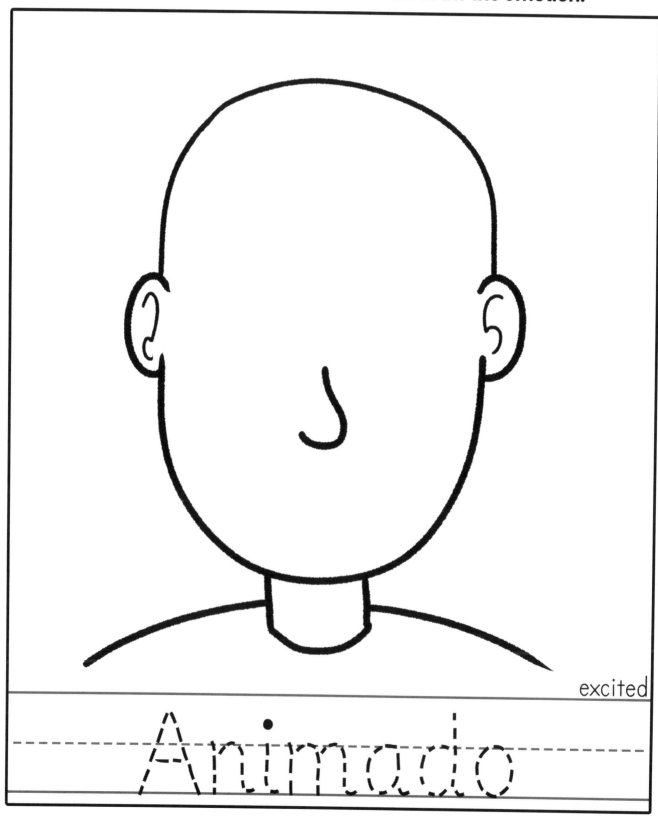

excited

Animado

Name: _____ Date: _____

Portuguese
Color the Alphabet

Wok
Wok

Portuguese
Color the Alphabet

Xilofone
Xylophone

How am I feeling?

Directions: Trace the word and then draw the emotion.

shy

Tímido

Portuguese
Color the Alphabet

Yoga
Yoga

How am I feeling?

Directions: Trace the word and then draw the emotion.

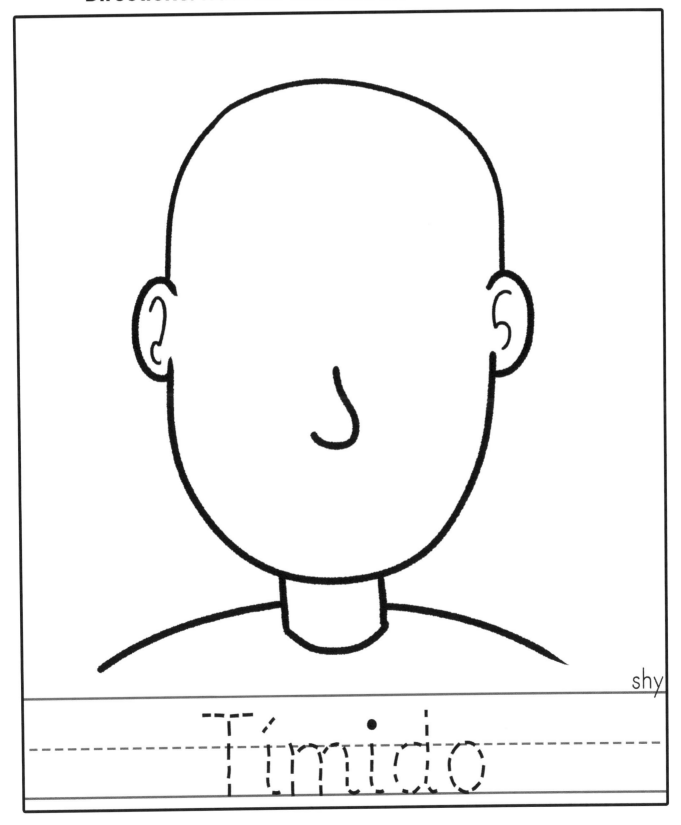

shy

Tímido

Name: _____   Date: _____

Portuguese
Color the Alphabet

Zebra
Zebra

How am I feeling?

Directions: Trace the word and then draw the emotion.

silly

Bobo

Thank you for learning with us!

doodles & safari

Choosing to teach your child at home can sometimes be a difficult decision for the family financially.

If you know a family in need that would love this book, please send me an email.

I will send you a PDF of this book with no questions asked.

doodlesafari@gmail.com

Made in the USA
Middletown, DE
19 December 2023

46375720R00057